DUAL ROLE

A Success Plan For Student Athletes

Elwood Scales III

ISBN: 0-9744719-0-9

Library of Congress Control Number: 2003096656

Printed in the United States by:
Morris Publishing
3212 East Highway 30
Kearney, NE 68847
1-800-650-7888

Dedication

This book is dedicated to all the men and women of the United States armed forces who are courageously serving in Afghanistan and Iraq.

Acknowledgements

To my Lord and Savior Jesus Christ,
thanks for your grace and mercy.

To my wife and son,
thanks for always giving me that one shining moment.

To my mom and dad,
thanks for patting me on my back when I failed and celebrating like two crazy people when I succeeded.

Pastor E. D. Richardson,
thanks for your anointed leadership and spirit-filled teachings.

Craig Shields, Eye Level Media + Design,
thanks for the graphic designs seen throughout this book, as well as being my brother-in-law.

Rodney Davenport, LIT Photography,
thanks for your cover photography work.

Laura Hill, Publishing Connections Inc.
thanks for your editorial and technical services.

To my many coaches and teammates through the years,
thanks for the fun and memories, which inspired this book.

Table of Contents

Introduction — *vii*

Chapter 1: What is a Student-Athlete? — *1*

Chapter 2: Don't Let Yesterday Determine Tomorrow — *8*

Chapter 3: Knowledge is Power — *13*

Chapter 4: Mind, Body and Soul — *18*

Chapter 5: Success is When Opportunity Meets Preparation — *24*

Chapter 6: Respect Everyone In and Around the Game — *29*

Chapter 7: Be a Class Act Off the Field — *35*

Chapter 8: When the Game is Over Move On — *42*

Athlete's Prayer — *49*

Selected References — *50*

Introduction

But seek first his kingdom and his righteousness, and all these things will be given to you as well.

Matthew 6:33

As a youth growing up in Wilmington, Delaware, I visualized dreams and had aspirations that most young males craved. During my high school years I experienced my share of challenges and setbacks, which I accepted and overcame. While in high school I participated in football, basketball and track. Although I planned to continue my athletic career at the college level, I soon realized that I was not one of the best. But if I had a chance to go to college, then who knows what the future might have in store.

I am the oldest of three children. My parents were very hard working and loving. Although I was rebellious at times, their continued love, support and guidance brought me a very long way and molded me into the person I am today.

Ironically, my enthusiasm for sports substantially exceeded my talent. Nevertheless, my high school coaches claimed they had contacts and knew people at the college level. They constantly stressed that if I kept my grades up and committed myself to them, they could get me a free ride to college. Once my senior year season came to an end, I thought I would be playing for a college team the following year. However, after repeated inquiries to my football and basketball coaches, I realized that I was left with a bunch of broken promises.

Since the efforts from my coaches were futile and I was complacent in the classroom, a college scholarship, at least in the near future, was out of the picture. My parents offered to send me to college, but I had settled in my mind that if I couldn't get a full athletic scholarship, than I would not go. With no other options available, I enlisted in the U.S. Air Force in 1980. With the

Lord's blessing, I was able to retire after 20 years of honorable service.

When I look back over my military career, I have no regrets whatsoever. It gave me the discipline and motivation I so desperately needed. I was able to earn three different degrees by taking advantage of the educational opportunities that were available. During my career I traveled to twenty different states and nine different countries, including a tour in the Persian Gulf. As an athlete, I have played basketball against some of the best national and international amateur teams. Last but not least, my military career enabled me to meet my beautiful wife Rhonda, who is my heart and soul.

Despite all these accolades and being born in the greatest country in the world, I still find my work undone. It saddens my heart to read the newspaper or to turn on the radio or television and hear about athletes jeopardizing their future with destructive behavior. It is not uncommon to hear about high school and college athletes getting involved in everything from academic fraud to violent crimes. The "dumb jock troublemaker" syndrome is at an all-time high. Despite the high tech society we live in, athletes are graduating from high school barely able to read and write. Some go on to college but, after completing four years of eligibility, they are going out into society with no marketable skills.

The Lord placed it in my heart to write this book to help combat this problem. There is no bona fide prescription for success. But, if you are a middle school, high school or college athlete and desire to be successful, then this book is written for you. Keep in mind that we control our own destiny and that winners aren't born, they are self-made.

What is a Student-Athlete?

Chapter 1

What is a Student-Athlete?

Everyone who competes in the games goes into strict training. They do it to get a crown that will not last; but we do it to get a crown that will last forever.

1 Corinthians 9:25

What is a student-athlete? Webster's Dictionary defines a *student* as a person formally engaged in learning, especially one enrolled in school or college. *Athlete* is defined as a person trained or gifted in exercises or contests involving physical agility, stamina, or strength. If you combine the two, a student-athlete is any student participating competitively in a sport of choice at a respective school. Whether you are in middle school playing football or in college playing golf, you fit the title of a student-athlete.

A successful life begins with a quality education. Your early commitment and understanding in elementary and middle school may set the foundation for your latter years. Advanced education is essential in today's job market. Unless you desire to wash dishes or flip burgers for a living, the days of getting a decent job with just a high school diploma are gone. College is not for everyone, but to succeed in a trade or vocation requires keeping up with the latest technology of this ever-changing world. Auto mechanics, plumbers and truck drivers are needed in our society just as much as doctors, lawyers and teachers. We are all blessed with different aptitudes and abilities that are needed in all areas of our economy and society. However, unless you are in a career you truly enjoy and you are making a difference in the lives of others, you may not experience true career success.

The student-athlete is consistently under scrutiny due to a history of poor academic performances. However, changes in academic requirements and a more serious approach to learning have improved this dilemma. Whether you are currently enrolled in middle school, high school, college or vocational school, your success will directly affect your future, as well as those around you.

Unfortunately, today some churches and religions speak out against athletic participation, believing that it is morally wrong and secular entertainment. However throughout the Bible athletic participation is discussed and encouraged in detail.

The following scriptures provide examples:

Among all these soldiers there were seven hundred chosen men who were left-handed, each of whom could sling a stone at a hair and not miss.

Judges 20: 16

Do you not know that in a race all the runners run, but only one gets the prize? Run in such a way as to get the prize.

Everyone who competes in the games goes into strict training. They do it to get a crown that will not last; but we do it to get a crown that will last forever.

Therefore I do not run like a man running aimlessly; I do not fight like a man beating the air.

No, I beat my body and make it my slave so that after I have preached to others, I myself will not be disqualified for the prize.

1 Corinthians 9:24-27

I went in response to a revelation and set before them the gospel that I preach among Gentiles. But I did this privately to those who seemed to be leaders, for fear that I was running or had run my race in vain.

Galatians 2:2

Similarly, if any one competes as an athlete, he does not receive the victor's crown unless he competes according to the rules.

2 Timothy 2:5

School sports have been important and continue to provide many benefits for youths. For starters, competitive sports help to provide healthy bodies and sound minds, which are essential in today's society due to the healthcare concerns that are ever-present. They also provide discipline, work ethic and teamwork, which are requirements for success in all walks of life. Some teenagers need sports as a safe haven and social outlet. *USA Today* newspaper recently reported that more youth crime and teenage sexuality occurs between the hours of 3:00 p.m. and 6:00 p.m. than any other portion of the day. Sports allow students to burn off energy and relieve daily frustrations, while at the same time keeping them off the streets. Participating in sports may also encourage students to be positive influences in their schools and communities.

As a working parent, it gives me extreme peace and comfort knowing that each afternoon when school lets out my eight year old son is at the YMCA shooting baskets or playing soccer. I would rather have him involved with athletic activities such as these, than coming home to an empty house and uncertain street corners.

Throughout history, man has invented games primarily as a means to meet socially with others, to display skills and physical ability, and to entertain or offer excitement. Most games involve some form of running, throwing, and jumping, all of which developed from basic hunting skills. As civilization shifted from a hunting and gathering base to a more settled farming community, it is likely that the carry-over of those activities formed the basis for the earliest games. Many early cultures, such as the Aztec Indians and the Greeks, incorporated religious and political elements into their games, but there was a desire for recreational play that eventually inspired the arrangement of early games and the invention of new ones.

Because early man relied heavily on running to hunt prey, foot races naturally developed and became the forerunner of track events. With the advent of the ball and bat, running became the basis for a wide range of modern games such as soccer, lacrosse (development of American Indian war skills), and field hockey. The ability to throw a killing tool far and accurately was transformed from a survival skill into a game skill (javelin throwing). The development of the bow and arrow not only added distance to the hunting throw, it also led to a variety of games, such as archery. Although no modern team game is based on solely jumping, the action is widely used as an adjunct in games, most notably in basketball and volleyball.

Early American settlers did not have time for modern day sports. More often than not, sports competition centered on work related chores such as baling hay, turkey shoots, and log-rolling or included the basic activities of swimming, boating, and fishing. There were, however, boxing matches, cockfights, and horse races to appeal to the interest of betting men.

The end of the Civil War in 1865 signaled the era when sports, as we know today, began to blossom. Boxing and baseball were two of the earliest big-time spectator sports. Tackle football started at the intercollegiate level in 1869, but did not begin its spurt of real growth until the turn of the century. Horse racing, rowing, and bicycling were sports that flourished, because they were identified with modes of transportation at the time. Golf and tennis were considered mostly "gentlemen's sports."

Spectator sports started becoming one of America's biggest pastimes after World War II. Once women were released from most household chores by modern appliances, and young girls were relieved of the male bias "tomboys," almost all Americans had opportunities to enjoy the sports their country had done so much to promote.

Also important in the development of games was the increasing urbanization of society. The emergence of towns with relatively stable populations permitted the organization of regular teams and schedules. As more teams entered into competition, however, conflicts arose as each team insisted on playing according to its own local standards. Thus, a uniform set of rules was made to regulate equipment and principles of play. Local and national organizations were also set up to govern the games, and a distinction was made between professional and amateur competitors.

Games serve a number of important functions. As physical outlets, they allow participants to work out violent energies and emotions that, if not thus channeled, may prove harmful to the community. As opportunities of display, games are accessible ways of gaining respect and admiration through the exhibition of skill. As entertainment, they provide diversion from the demands of day-to-day living and allow the spectator to enjoy much of the experience of play without actual involvement. In addition, the economic impact of games is unquestionable. Several of the most popular games have become major industries worldwide.

American intercollegiate competition is a phenomenon in itself. Major colleges and universities generate huge profits and have multi-million dollar budgets. Some collegiate football stadiums seat up to 100,000 fans and basketball arenas with capacities for 10,000 to 15,000 people. Athletes are not considered professional at the college level, but many receive free tuition and living expenses.

Title IX has helped girls and women participate in interscholastic and intercollegiate athletics in far greater numbers than they had in the past. In 1971, Title IX was enacted as a federal law which opened the doors for female athletes to obtain equal scholarship opportunities and long deserved recognition. Girls and women also are increasingly participants in sports that have traditionally been seen as off limits such as lacrosse, wrestling, soccer, rugby and ice hockey. One sport that has become a favorite for young girls is soccer; the results have led to a World Cup championship. In 1996, the U.S. National Soccer Team captured the first-ever women's Olympic medal in soccer before a crowd of 76,481. In doing so its position as the world's premier women's soccer program was established.

In many ways, the image of American women in the sports arena is being redefined by the many accomplishments of women athletes. Women are now seen as sports stars in their own right, from Mia Hamm in soccer to Sheryl Swoopes in basketball. The inspiring story of Dr. Dot Richardson, the captain of the American Olympic softball team, who immediately left her triumph in Atlanta to begin her medical residency, exemplifies just what has been accomplished on the field and off as a result of Title IX.

While growing up Dot never believed that playing baseball was reserved for boys. She went on to become a four-time All-American in college and was named NCAA player of the decade for the 1980s. She graduated as a physician from the University of Louisville Medical School, often ending 20-hour hospital shifts with workouts and practice so that she could compete in 1996 in the first women's softball appearance in the modern Olympic Games. She hit the first home run in Olympic softball history, helping the U.S. team win the gold medal. Dot is now a resident in orthopedic surgery at the University of Southern California.

"Without Title IX, I'd be nowhere."
-Cheryl Miller, Olympic athlete and sports commentator-

There are various competitive sports at the middle school, high school and college levels. Your desire, background, and physical characteristics will determine which sport is best suited for you. Unfortunately, some sports do not receive the publicity, capacity crowds, and news headlines that other sports receive. However, the same level of teamwork and competitiveness is still there. If you go into any high school or college gymnasium that has championship programs, it doesn't take long to notice that the banners on the wall are all the same size and the same color whether they're for football, swimming or golf.

I remember once reading an article in *Sports Illustrated* about current Iowa State head wrestling coach Bobby Douglas. Prior to his arrival at Iowa State, he had coached the wrestling program at Arizona State where his teams literally owned the Pacific Conference. His teams were conference champions nine times and brought home the NCAA title in 1988. In the article he said "wrestling will never bring in the money that football and basketball brings, all it can do is help turn out the right individual." He has since taken his philosophy and winning ways to Iowa State where he continually expects total commitment from his athletes on the mat, in the classroom and in the community. He has produced numerous All-Americans and his teams are consistently nationally ranked in the top ten every year. While traveling throughout the country competing in numerous invitational tournaments, his athletes are often seen using airport terminals as study halls for such demanding majors as business administration and engineering. One does not have to be a genius to realize that the athletes of this program thrive on competition and quality education.

Today's sports have become multi-million dollar enterprises. Unfortunately, high school and college sports are often treated as a business, rather than a game. Illegal recruiting, exploitation and gambling are increasingly the norm. Fortunately, every student-athlete is in a position to make a difference. If you keep the Lord first and foremost in everything you do, then you will be victorious in the end regardless of the sport or final score. Whether it is on the playing field, in the classroom or in the community, today's student-athletes are in a position to be role models to children and their peers alike. Regardless of who you are and where you are as long as you compete hard and compete fair, you should get the rewards and recognition worthy of a student-athlete.

Don’t Let Yesterday Determine Tomorrow

Chapter 2

Don't let Yesterday Determine Tomorrow

Brothers, I do not consider myself yet to have taken hold of it. But one thing I do: Forgetting what is behind and striving toward what is ahead, I press on toward the goal to win the prize for which God has called me heavenward in Christ Jesus.
Philippians 3:13-14

With the exception of Jesus Christ, no one has ever lived a perfect life. Whether you are a student-athlete or not, everyone has misjudged, fallen short and failed at one time or another. We have a choice either to let shortcomings of the past continue to haunt and burden us or to use them as stepping stones for a confidence-filled and prosperous future. Many successful business leaders, politicians and entertainers have come from less than humble beginnings and have gone on to achieve great things with their lives. Whether it is poverty, depression, or run-ins with the law, we serve an almighty God who is merciful and will look past our faults and see our needs, if we only humble ourselves.

In this day and age it hurts me to hear any young person speak negatively about what they can or cannot do. Have you heard of someone who was always perceived as a loser, but as time passed things suddenly changed for the better. Do you know someone who performed poorly in the classroom throughout middle school, but became a honor student in high school. There have been reserve players in high school who walked on a college sports team and earned a scholarship.

Ironically, it works both ways. The person who was voted Most Likely to Succeed may end up living a marginal life. Although the star athlete may be most popular in high school, his/her collegiate career may not pan out. If something didn't work out in the past, it should never destroy your future goals or dreams. If you still have breath in your body and have use of your mind and limbs, then you should never let setbacks of the past darken your future.

While growing up Rodney Cummings attended 27 different grade schools. His mother was a drug addict and prostitute. His father couldn't afford to take care of him as a teenager. In 1973, Cummings was a wayward 18 year old who had just served two weeks in an Indiana jail for burglary and was later sentenced to three years probation. While walking home from the Madison County jail, after being released on his own recognizance, Cummings walked past the Anderson Police Athletic League (PAL) club, which had just opened. Shortly thereafter, he joined and started boxing. This decision became a turning point in his life. Cummings would later win three Indiana Golden Gloves titles and a college scholarship, which he used to attend Ball State University.

As a result of the positive influence of police officers at the PAL club, he soon had aspirations of becoming a police officer. In 1979 he petitioned and received a pardon from the governor so he could become a police officer. After receiving his bachelor's degree, he earned his master's and law degrees, became a decorated police officer, and joined the prosecutor's office in the same county where he found himself on the wrong side of the law as a youth. Today, Cummings serves as the Madison County Prosecuting Attorney and, in an ironic twist, was elected over the same official who sought his conviction nearly 30 years earlier.

Cummings doesn't consider himself a rags-to-riches story. He credits the opportunity for higher education and the police officers at the PAL club for keeping him off the streets and saving his life. "I don't like hearing excuses," Cummings said. "If you sit around and start feeling sorry for yourself, you'll never make it."

-Use a setback as a setup for a comeback-

When I was in tenth grade I was cut from my high school basketball team. I took it hard because of my love for the game and for the first time since fifth grade I wouldn't be playing competitively for a team. As a 6'2" 14 yearold, I felt that I should have made the team. I went home defeated and disappointed. Later I was teased and taunted by individuals who made the team and other students in the school.

My father stressed that I could not change what had happened and that I could choose between staying depressed, which would eventually affect my academics and personal life, or work twice as hard over the summer to improve my skills to prove that coach and everyone else wrong. I chose to do the latter.

You don't have to be a genius to realize that nothing is guaranteed and that life changes every day. The following year the school district where I went to high school was rezoned, which meant the school had an additional 150 students added to its enrollment. I was fortunate to make the team during my junior year, despite a new coach and increased competition from the larger student body. Most of the guys who made the team during my sophomore year did not go out for the team during my junior year. There were a few guys from the previous season who started out with the team, but for one reason or another they chose to quit before the season ended. During my junior year I played sparingly, but I had fun and it also prepared me for the next year.

I continued to work hard over the next summer by doing a lot of individual drills I learned while attending camps and playing in summer leagues. When my senior year arrived I finally cracked the starting lineup. Shortly after making the starting lineup I crossed paths with the coach who had cut me when I was a sophomore. He was coaching at another high school, which we had played against early in the season. As fate would have it, I had the best game of my high school career that night. I ended up with 15 points, 12 rebounds and 5 blocks. But most important, we won and won big!

The lessons I learned are first, by not making the team my sophomore year I could have easily become discouraged, intimidated and chose not to play any more, which I have seen happen to so many people. Second, it took two years to get the break that I deserved, and still some continued to have doubts in my abilities. But, I never doubted myself which resulted in me proving them all wrong in the end.

There are three things I want to emphasize in this chapter.

1. Just because you play or do not play on a team one year doesn't guarantee **anything** the next year. All it takes is an injury, academic ineligibility, dismissal, or complacency to turn a starting spot into a roster vacancy. Things can drastically change in a short period of time. For example, when I didn't make the team during my sophomore year there were 17 guys who played in that program (junior varsity and varsity) as underclassman (sophomores and juniors). However, of those 17 only two of them and myself successfully completed our high school careers as seniors.
2. When I got cut from the basketball team I experienced a lot of taunting and ridicule from some of the guys who made the team. Ironically, within a year our roles had reversed. Rather than taunting and ridiculing in return, I chose to put the past behind me and enjoy the opportunity. That experience alone taught me to *never* look down on another person regardless of any circumstance, because roles can literally reverse overnight. The same fate or misfortune that you may wish on someone can come back to haunt you. Whether it is sports, academics or circumstances, if you can't say anything positive and encouraging it's better not to say anything at all. As the old sayings goes "your day shall come" or "what goes around comes around."
3. Most importantly if you fail at something, never give up.

   National Basketball Association Hall of Famer Nate "Tiny" Archibald has the distinction of being the only person in history to lead the NBA in both scoring and assists in the same season. However, few people know that he didn't make his high school team until his senior year. It's a safe bet that he doesn't want to imagine what could have happened if he had chosen to quit after the first time he didn't make the team.

   Alexander Graham Bell failed many times and was told to abandon his idea before he finally invented the telephone. Can you imagine how difficult our lives would be today if he chose to quit after his early failures? I know it would be pretty hard trying to stay in touch with family and friends by telegraph or mail. Remember, if you want something badly enough and you are willing to work for it with all your heart and soul and seek guidance from the Lord, it shall be granted according to Mathew 6:33, which states "But seek first His kingdom and His righteousness; and all these things shall be added to you."

As my Little League coach would say "a winner never quits and a quitter never wins."

"The past cannot be changed, the future is still in your power"

-Hugh White-

Knowledge is Power

Chapter 3

Knowledge is Power

Study to show thyself approved unto God, a workman that needeth not be ashamed, rightly dividing to word of truth.
2 Timothy 2:15

Every young athlete has dreamed at least once in his or her life about being a professional athlete. Unfortunately, the odds are against this becoming a reality for most athletes. A recent study quoted in ESPN Magazine stated that you can fill Giant Stadium with 50,000 high school athletes, but only one of the 50,000 will reach the professional ranks. This means there are going to be a lot of disappointed athletes year-in and year-out unless they have a backup plan, which is education.

Education is so essential during and after your playing days. Obviously, everyone cannot be a Rhodes Scholar, but keep in mind that high standards of academics are needed to be and stay eligible for your respective sport. Education is needed for most advanced and high paying jobs. In the past a person could learn some vocational skills through on-the-job training. Today local community colleges that offer certifications for skills such as electronics and welding also require English 101 for curriculum completion. This is understandable because most employers and customers wouldn't want a technician or mechanic using equipment or performing a service without proper knowledge or understanding of the task at hand.

College is not for everyone, but if you choose to pursue that route it will require much discipline and commitment to succeed. To become a disciplined student the work ethic should start as early as elementary school. However regardless of the level you're presently at, you can achieve academic success. There are high school dropouts who later went on to earn GEDs and college degrees. You must be willing to work just as hard or harder in the classroom as you do on the playing field in order to secure a bright future. Most honor roll students credit success to dedication and sacrifice rather than natural ability. Dedication and sacrifice go hand-in-hand and, when teamed up, can be the difference between success and failure.

You must be willing to accept full responsibility for your destiny. Most teenagers want to be accepted by others. However other people can't always get you where you want to go. Sometimes you may have to give up hanging out with friends or talking on the phone in order to complete an assignment. Sometimes you may have to stay up late and miss what's on television to get in needed study time. Sometimes you must be willing to meet with teachers before or after school to get help in difficult courses. And, do not be too proud to ask other exceptional students for assistance, even if they are not athletes. If you are serious and sincere, most students will be honored to help if asked.

Practice makes perfect. This serves true for everything from knowing history events to doing mathematical equations. The more you recite, write or calculate something, the easier it comes to memory. Keep in mind there are always rules to various types of writing and math. Know the rules and the rest should become second nature. If you have a walkman to listen to your favorite recording artists, use that same walkman to listen to prerecorded study notes from classes and homework assignments. There is plenty of time and opportunity to listen to these tapes such as: walking to school, riding to games or just sitting around relaxing.

Every student should have a personal library card from the local public library. There is no other place where you can find so much information and knowledge under one roof. Whatever you want and need to learn about you can find it at your local public library. Whether it is learning about computers, speaking a foreign language or needing to know more about prominent world figures. All it takes is a trip to the library. The library is a good resource for school assignments.

When I was a teenager and young adult I would go to the library on some Saturday afternoons to read the latest issues of magazines. It was a good way to pass time, while keeping up with the latest trends, events and whatever subjects peaked my interest. Most importantly, this wealth of knowledge and resources was acquired at government expense and doesn't cost *anything!*

Finally, to make the package complete, the student-athlete should study the Bible because it is the ultimate source for guidance and successful living. You are never too young to be well-versed in the Bible. There are Bible translations available from children's versions to theologians. Every man, woman, boy and girl should study the Bible on a daily basis. My pastor, Rev. E. D. Richardson of New Beginning Ministry in Hampton, Virginia suggests 20-30 minutes each day as a minimum. To make study time more effective you should study early in the morning when the day begins because, during this part of the day the mind is fresh and distractions are at a minimum. This will also allow you throughout the day to reflect on what you learned, as well as share it with others. If you are a beginner, use a study Bible which translates complex biblical terms into simple everyday language. Other tools that are essential for effective Bible studies are a concordance, dictionary and a highlighter. These tools will allow you to research, define and caption significant events and individuals throughout the Bible.

If allotting time each day for Bible study is a challenge, another option is reading devotional literature, such as *Daily Bread* and *The Upper Room.* Taking a few minutes each day to read these guides, along with referenced scriptures, will help build a solid foundation in your spiritual growth. For your casual reading consider *Sharing the Victory* and *Sports Spectrum,* which are magazines profiling the lifestyles of Christian athletes.

One prime example of the ideal student-athlete is current NFL quarterback Danny Wuerffel. While at the University of Florida, Wuerffel won the Heisman Trophy and national championship in 1996. He also was the recipient of numerous academic awards. While in college he often led Bible studies in his dorm room, which changed the lives of many of his teammates for the better. He contributes his success to his faith in God and hard work on the field and in the classroom. A person with the right priorities and purpose should have a bright future.

Guide to Homework and Successful Studying

10 Strategies for Homework Success

1. Write down all assignments as they are given. Immediately place assignments in a notebook, the one and only place, where all assignments are kept.
2. Begin homework at the same time everyday.
3. Pick a quiet place and sit in a hard back chair at a table or desk. DO NOT try to study on your bed, sprawled out on the couch, etc. There should be no distractions.
4. Never try to study and watch television or listen to the radio or CD's at the same time.
5. Do not answer the telephone during study periods. All calls should be taken by someone else who will explain that you are studying and can't be disturbed. You can return calls later. This includes calls about the homework. Be honest, these calls are generally social, and rarely assist in getting work done.
6. Before you start to study, gather all the things you will need. Sharpen your pencils, have plenty of paper, get all your books and homework assignments, and be ready to work.
7. After you think you have memorized something, spend more time studying it. Under test pressure, it's often more difficult to remember things than you may have thought.
8. When you get an assignment that is not due for several days (or even weeks) work on it at least 15 minutes every night starting from the first day you got the assignment, until it is complete.
9. Read for pleasure every day. Pick a favorite book, a newspaper, magazine. Try to challenge yourself.
10. Write every day. Get a notebook and write a page a day. Write about your goals, your life, what you need to do, what

makes you happy, upset, sad, cry. It doesn't matter what you write about, just write.

There is no such thing as not having homework.

Not having homework may mean a student is failing or underachieving. If a student really thinks there is not homework, any of the following can be used for studying:

a. Reread any textbook or literature, rework any problems or work sheets, and rewrite any paper or assignment. You may also read ahead in your reading material.

b. When in doubt, see your teacher and ask for ideas on what to study.

c. Go to library and check out three books related to your subjects and read them during your study time.

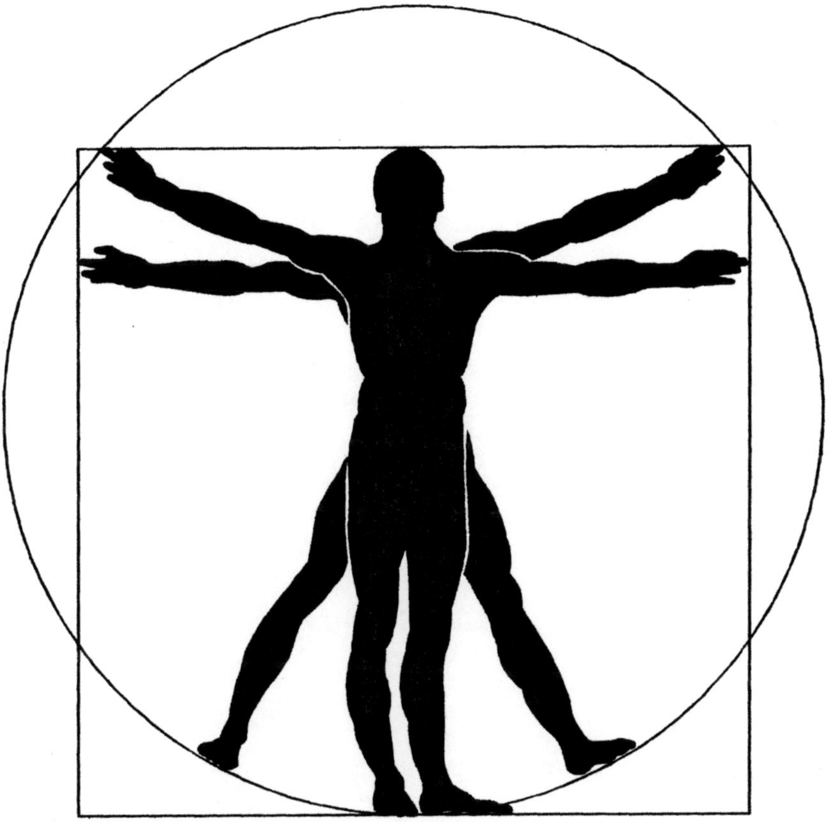

Mind, Body and Soul

Chapter 4

Mind, Body and Soul

What? Know ye not that your body is a temple of the Holy Ghost which is in you, which ye have of God, and ye are not your own?
1 Corinthians 6:19

In order to excel in the classroom and on the playing field your mind must be sound and your body must be in peak condition. We are born with only one body, unfortunately it doesn't come with any warranty or interchangeable parts. One of the best defenses against diseases and infections is the body's resistance to illness. Staying in top physical condition and observing a high standard of hygiene will reduce the risk of diseases and infections.

The key to maintaining our bodies is controlling what goes into it and how it is used. In this chapter we will examine significant factors that influence how well your body performs, such as diet, tobacco, alcohol, and drug use, hygiene and rest.

Diet

As the architect of your athletic and academic career, you are responsible for insuring that you eat well-planned and balanced meals. Even if you do not cook your own meals, you should select your foods wisely and offer suggestions about what your meals should include. The following information from the U.S. Department of Agriculture and the Food and Drug Administration will help you do both.
Your diet should supply your body with seven basic nutrients: protein, carbohydrates, fats, vitamins, minerals, fiber and water.

Proteins are necessary for such functions as building and repairing body tissue, for the production of antibodies, enzymes, hormones, and hemoglobin, and for use as a reserve energy source. Meat, fish, eggs, poultry, milk, cheese and peanut butter are high quality sources of protein.

Carbohydrates supply energy as the body's primary fuel. Cereals, grains, potatoes, fruits, vegetables, sugar and breads are major sources of carbohydrates.

Saturated fats are a source of reserve energy and are essential to the body for proper growth. Sources of saturated fats are butter, margarine, cooking and salad oils, meats and dairy products. However, excessive amounts of fats in the diet can lead to a variety of health problems.

Vitamins play an important role in the body process, such as converting energy from foods, promoting health tissue growth, and aiding the normal function of the nerves and muscles. A well-balanced diet will provide a good supply of the vitamins needed by the body each day.

Minerals help the body perform numerous vital functions and maintain healthy tissues. Calcium is the most abundant mineral in the body and helps maintain strong teeth and bones. Iron is necessary for the blood to carry oxygen and carbon dioxide to and from the cells.

Fiber is added to the diet from such sources as the stems of salad greens, celery, wheat bran, apple skins and raisins. Fiber is necessary for normal action of the intestinal tract and the removal of waste from the body.

Water makes up about two-thirds of the body and is essential for life. Water is taken into the body from many sources such as liquids, fruits, vegetables, meats and even breads. The body needs at least sixty-four ounces (eight glasses) of water each day. One of the simplest ways to stay healthy is to drink plenty of water. Water helps to regulate our temperature, to protect our joints, to keep our vital organs functioning properly and even to fight off certain types of cancer.

Planning your meals. The following suggestions offer a balanced diet with a variety of foods:

Breakfast
Fruit or juice – fresh, canned or frozen
Cereal – ready to eat or cooked
Protein – meat, eggs, bacon, ham or sausage

Bread – hot cakes, waffles, French toast, or toast
Beverage – milk is the best choice

Lunch and Dinner
Soup or salad with dressing
Protein – one or more servings per meal
Vegetables – select two or more per meal
Bread or rolls – with butter or margarine
Desert – fresh fruit, cookies, cake, ice cream, etc.
Beverage – milk, fruit juice, iced tea or water

It is especially important that you start each day with a good, balanced breakfast. If you don't have time for breakfast, start getting up earlier. If no one will fix balanced meals for you, learn to fix them yourself. You are responsible for your own academic and athletic success; eating a well planned and balanced diet will increase your chances of reaching your goals.

Suggested Snacks
Carrot sticks, celery sticks, fruits, raisins, peanuts, pretzels, cereal bars, popcorn (no salt or butter) and yogurt provide nutrition and help maintain energy levels, if a snack is needed between meals.

Tobacco (cigarettes and snuff) reduces breathing capacity and the body's ability to absorb oxygen. Tobacco is considered a factor in lung and mouth cancer. Recent medical studies have also determined that smoking causes tooth decay and gum disease.

Alcohol and Drug Use

Alcohol (beer, wine, and liquor) impairs judgement and motor skills. Prolonged use causes damage to the stomach, kidneys and liver.

Drugs (narcotics) produce irritations and damage to the brain, heart and nervous system. Also, the long-term use of drugs can increase the risk of serious health problems, lead to physical and mental addiction, decrease the body's ability to fight infection and cause death. Last, but not least, they are *illegal!*

Steroids (performance enhancing drugs) despite claims of fast gains in muscle strength, size and weight, the use of steroids can lead to liver and kidney damage, sterilization, cancer and death.

Despite arguments to the contrary, these substances can hurt your performance in sports by decreasing your ability to compete and put forth a 100 % effort. Because all sports are games of inches, of hundredths of seconds, of calculated risks, and of seized opportunities, it is ridiculous to believe that over time drugs will not reduce your strength, slow your speed, and warp your judgement just enough to cause you to be, at best, several inches short or a few seconds too slow to come out a winner.

It may be true that most of the people who experiment with drugs end up relatively unaffected, leave the drugs behind, and go on with the rest of their lives. But the effects of drug use vary widely from person to person and are largely unpredictable. Accidents, problems, and addictions don't always happen to the other person. You have so much to lose if you get arrested for drug possession or Driving While Intoxicated (DWI), which very easily could lead to the loss of your life or that of others. I am aware of many people who were heavy drug users and drinkers and were successfully rehabilitated. These people went on to live clean and sober lives, but experienced serious health problems as a result of their past addictions.

CNN recently reported that during the 2001, 72 % of all violent crimes (murder, rape, assault, and robbery) that occurred on college campuses involved the use of alcohol and drugs. There is no logical reason why anyone should sacrifice his or her long-term success for alcohol or drugs.

You are responsible for yourself and your own success. This responsibility extends beyond the weight room, the locker room and the playing field. Everything you do today will drastically influence the kind of student-athlete and the kind of person you become. Don't jeopardize your present and future with alcohol or drugs.

Personal Hygiene is the most essential step to good grooming and good health. Everyday cleanliness is common knowledge. Practicing good personal hygiene will drastically help you reduce contracting bacteria and infections. More often than you know, good looks are the result of careful and continuous grooming. The following suggestions will assist you in maintaining your good health:

- Visit your doctor and dentist annually.
- Brush your teeth and gargle at least twice a day with an antiseptic mouthwash. Floss daily, preferably at bedtime.
- Shower or bathe at least once a day. Use deodorant/antiperspirant.
- Moisturize your skin and hair daily.
- Wash hands before each meal and when necessary, this is the single best method of infection control.
- Change clothes and socks daily.

Sex outside of marriage is unscriptural. Inappropriate sexual use of your body can result in socially transmitted diseases and unwanted pregnancies. AIDS and HIV are running rampant in American and killing people of all ages and races. Despite societie's claims of safe sex, teenagers are increasingly getting pregnant and infected. The safest sex is abstinence.

Sleep and food are the two essentials that allow you to live. Adequate sleep gives your mind and body a chance to perform daily maintenance and repairs. Studies have shown that only half of the people in the United States get proper sleep each night. Try to get seven to eight hours each night. And to ensure proper rest, go to sleep and get up at the same time every day.

Laugh once a day—at least. The act of laughing has so many benefits from both an emotional and physical perspective. Respiration and circulation are both enhanced through the act of laughter. We oxygenate the blood, which energizes us and helps us think more clearly. Letting out a good laugh stimulates chemicals in the brain that actually suppress stress-related hormones. So what it comes down to is that a good laugh each day will help you live longer.

Transform Stress into Power

Stress can be harmful and may lead to heart disease, ulcers or high blood pressure.

4 Skills for managing stress:

1. *Awareness:* Identify stressors (headaches, fatigue, impatience, anger, depression and overeating).
2. *Acceptance:* Find ways to accept what cannot be changed. Keep things in perspective. Use positive self-talk. Consider problems as challenges, constantly pray and seek guidance when necessary.
3. *Coping:*
   *Stay active – Exercise reduces depression and stress.
   *Relax – True relaxation involves skills you can learn, like deep breathing, or treating yourself to healthy rewards such as a good walk or a hot bath.
4. *Action skills:* Talk with your family and friends. Set priorities and manage your time wisely.

Remember that the Lord only blessed you with one body and its up to you to take care of it, enjoy it and use it to His glory.

Success is when Opportunity meets Preparation

Chapter 5

Success is When Opportunity Meets Preparation

But as for you, be strong and do not give up, for your work will be rewarded.

2 Chronicles 15:7

People who maximize their potential are considered a success. But success doesn't happen overnight. It requires preparation. If you compete without training or pursue a job without having the proper knowledge, skills and abilities, it is safe to say that you will probably lose out every time. Most opportunities that come in our lives usually come without warning. Being prepared will help you make the most of any opportunity that comes your way. Having a positive attitude and a good work ethic will also help prepare you for anticipated opportunities.

While growing up I was once told, "if you ever want to see a perfect example of good work ethic in action just visit the rear kitchen of any Chinese food restaurant. Upon viewing this you will see planning, individual determination and team work at its finest." The end results are satisfied customers and lucrative profits.

The late track and field Olympian Florence Griffith Joyner used a disappointing second-place finish in the 1984 Olympic games as fuel for the fire. "Second place wasn't good enough," she said with an attitude. "I decided that I was going for three gold medals in the 1988 games, and I knew what it would take to reach my goal." What did it take? Let's count the cost. It took discipline, hard work and sheer desire as she relentlessly maintained a rigorous training schedule. Every morning she would run at the crack of dawn before going to work at a bank. Her afternoons were filled with even more sprints followed by stretching, strength exercises and weight lifting. And if that wasn't enough, when money got low she squeezed more hours into an already hectic schedule by moonlighting as a beautician at area beauty salons. Day after day, month after month, she maintained this grueling routine for four years!

Was it worth the effort? Absolutely! At the 1988 Olympics in Seoul, Korea she won three gold medals, earning the title of the "world's fastest woman." Almost as famous for her muscular physique, her flamboyant style, particularly her six-inch-long polished fingernails, allowed her to capture so many hearts with her winning style. Until her sudden death in 1998 at age 38, Florence Griffith Joyner, known as "FloJo" was a media sensation and an inspiration to others simply because she desired to be the best.

Due to the growing popularity of school sports, today's athletes can take advantage of opportunities at the middle school and high school levels with no limitations except an athlete's enthusiasm and his or her desire to improve. For many athletes, the solid foundation of their sports knowledge begins and ends with what their coaches have told them and what they have learned on television. As soon as these athletes leave the playing field, they normally forget everything until the next practice. They know their roles and where they are supposed to be, but every thing else seems to escape them.

When an athlete's knowledge of a sport and of athletics in general increases, his or her performances and overall career will be greatly enhanced. There is no greater source of information than the public library. The library has dozens of books for the serious athlete from learning fundamentals and techniques to biographies and autobiographies. There are several good magazines available that provide current information, as well as good inside looks at different sports.

Your knowledge of a sport can make the difference in what positions you play and in the responsibilities you have during games. To become a team captain or a team leader, you must know more than the average go-with-the flow players. Your sports knowledge will aid in a smoother transition from middle school to high school or from junior college to college. If a selection is close, a coach or recruiter will generally choose a sharper athlete, because he or she is more likely to be an asset to the team. Camps and clinics are another way to get personal instruction to improve your skills for you respective sport. If you are willing to learn more than what the coach advises you and what you see on television, you will be surprised at how much your performance improves.

Through years of talking to coaches and athletes, I learned that coaches love leaders and team players. They love the person who runs to be the first in line to start practice drills. They love the person who is vocal and tries to keep the rest of the team motivated during practice, games and matches. They love the person who is receptive to criticism and is willing to work harder to improve weaknesses. They love the person who puts the team before himself/herself. Finally, they love the person who is willing to work in the off-season just as hard as they do during the regular season. All these attributes add up to the ideal athlete that every coach would want on their team.

The only place where success comes before work is in the dictionary

Larry Bird is considered by most as the best small forward to play in the National Basketball Association. While playing for the Boston Celtics, the team won three NBA championships and Larry Bird received three Most Valuable Player awards. He was also a member of the Olympian Dream Team that brought home a gold medal from the 1992 Olympics in Barcelona. But if you were to ask any of his former teammates what he was best known for most, if not all, will remember his tireless work ethic. During his playing career Larry was always the first person to arrive at practice and usually the last one to leave. Sometimes he was there early shooting jump shots or staying late running the steps in the Boston Garden Arena. He always felt there was something extra he could do to improve his game.

His teammates were so fascinated by his attitude, hard work and determination that it inspired them to work harder and win championships. When Larry Bird first came into the NBA some doubted that he would become a superstar, because he was slow and didn't play above the rim. Throughout his stellar career he continually used his strengths to his advantage by mastering basic fundamentals, out hustling and out thinking his opponents. Larry Bird will go down in history as one of the greatest simply because he refused to let anyone out work him.

One day as I was driving home from work listening to a local radio station, I heard Coach Patricia Bibbs, the women's basketball coach at Hampton University being interviewed and answering telephone calls over the air. She received compliments from various callers concerning her team's recent success, which included a conference championship and NCAA tournament appearance. One caller mentioned to Coach Bibbs that she played basketball in high school and was a freshman at the university. She wanted to tryout for the team as a walk-on during the upcoming season and wanted to know what was required. Coach Bibbs responded by announcing when the tryouts would take place and stressing that it's the athlete's responsibility to be in top shape, physically and mentally, on the first day of practice. If the athlete doesn't know what they have to do in the off-season, they should contact the respective coach to obtain an off-season conditioning workout program and follow it religiously.

Wrestling great Dan Gable once said that each time he learned a new wrestling move he would practice it at least 100 times! Some may think of this as going to the extreme, but, if you want to out perform your opposition, you must be willing to out work them. What did thousands of road miles and thousands of training hours do for Dan Gable? For starters, while in college he had a record of 100 straight wins against one defeat. His lone defeat came during the last match of his senior year, which he would later avenge. During the 1972 Munich Olympics he defeated six straight opponents without surrendering one single point, ultimately bringing home the gold medal. So it's safe to say that he successfully prepared himself for all opportunities that came his way.

Keep in mind that some opportunities will take longer to come than others. You may have to wait months or even years for your opportunity to come. It is not uncommon in high school and college to be in a program two or three years before you get a chance to play or compete. Regardless of the circumstances, it is important that you always stay focused and prepare for the future.

St. Louis Rams Quarterback Kurt Warner serves as a prime example of patience and preparation. Despite having an excellent high school football career, he only received a partial scholarship to Northern Iowa. After being forced to sit out his first year, he did not start until he was a fifth year senior. After being drafted and cut by the Green Bay Packers in 1994, he stacked shelves in a grocery store followed by stints in the Arena Football League and NFL Europe respectively.

After making the Rams as a third string quarterback in 1997, he continued to run, lift weights and throw passes in the off-season while waiting for bigger opportunities. As fate would have it, at the start of the 1998 season the 1st and 2nd string Rams quarterbacks went down with injuries. Upon starting as quarterback, he guided the Rams all the way through the season, the playoffs and eventually the Super Bowl title. During the 1999 season he led the NFL in numerous passing categories and earned NFL and Super Bowl MVP honors.

Kurt, who is a devout Christian, never lost focus of his dreams and ambitions despite numerous setbacks early in his career. He consistently quotes "all things are possible with Jesus." He was definitely able to succeed when his preparation met his opportunity.

Respect Everyone In and Around The Game

Chapter 6

Respect Everyone In and Around the Game

And we urge you, brothers, warn those who are idle, encourage the timid, help the weak, be patient with everyone.
1 Thessalonians 5:14

To be a respectable athlete you must compete with true sportsmanship. Unfortunately this is lacking in most professional sports due to egos, violence and financial demands. Sportsmanship is the ability to play fair. A good sport can lose without complaining and win without gloating. Displaying true sportsmanship brings more grace and glamour to sports than talent and skill will ever do. Tennis great Jimmy Connors once stated " true sportsmanship is when two individuals play a hard fought match and at the end no one can tell who won or lost."

Every athlete has lost at one time or another. And every athlete has had setbacks, failures, and disappointments. Baseball legend Babe Ruth struck out more often than he hit homeruns. The Denver Broncos lost four of six Super Bowls. Boxing legend Muhammad Ali won and lost the heavyweight championship three times. No matter how good you become, there will always be wins and losses, peaks and valleys. The important thing is how you feel about yourself after the losses and disappointments, and what you do to overcome them. It's easy to be a good winner. Anyone can hold their head high after a big victory. The challenge lies in overcoming the defeats and disappointments and achieving your goals just the same.

When you make the decision to compete seriously in athletics, you take on three principal responsibilities: 1) to do everything you can in practice and training to develop your skills and abilities to the highest possible level; 2) to make the greatest effort you can in actual competition to insure that you perform your best and win the contest; and 3) to practice good sportsmanship at all times. No one can ask you to do more. In fact, if you fulfill these responsibilities diligently, while striving for excellence in everything you do, you will always be able to hold your head up high and feel good about yourself. Regardless of your win/loss record, your sports career will be a success, and you can be just as proud of your accomplishments as any world champion.

Showing respect and courtesy for all says a lot about you as an athlete and as a person. Athletes, coaches and officials are needed to make any athletic contest possible. Without these individuals you cannot compete and have fun.

Coaches

I once saw a poster in a high school gym that read "A good coach improves your game, a great coach improves your life." There are good and bad coaches at all levels. The most common ingredient of good coaching is the ability to teach. Some of the very best athletes credit their success to good coaching throughout their careers. Bad coaching can involve favoritism, the inability to relate to athletes and an overemphasis on sports. Whatever situation you may be placed in, always treat your coaches with the utmost respect and accept their decisions regardless of how you or others may feel. Do not question their decisions or whom they decide to play. Do not speak negatively about your coaches when they are not around and also discourage others from doing so. Obey your coaches and give them 100%, win or lose. Coaches have tremendous pressure on them. And if a team isn't winning, the coach is usually the first one to go.

University of Tennessee Women's Basketball Coach Pat Summitt has brought home the NCAA championship six times during her tenure. Despite the success her teams have achieved, she stresses and demands personal responsibility from all her players. Coach Summitt makes it a policy to meet with her players, individually, four times a year to discuss everything from athletics and academic status to family and career goals.

During these meetings she is open to any questions and comments and provides any needed guidance and referrals.

Even though we are all responsible for our own success, it is possible that you may need your high school or college coach to help you get to the next level or provide a job reference. You don't have to be a superstar or the coaches' pet, but if you are loyal and work hard coaches' will usually want to help you whenever they can. At season's end, regardless of how successful the team was, always let the coach know that you had fun and enjoyed playing for him or her.

Teammates

You should always try to consider your teammates as your extended family. Most athletes and coaches will agree that the team that is closer and more personal has an advantage once they step on the field. Never put one another down when someone makes a mistake, especially if they are on the field hustling their heart out because mistakes are inevitable. If you are vying for playing time against someone who is playing in front of you, the quickest way into any coaches' doghouse is to criticize a teammate. The best approach is to out work that person, along with everyone else, and leave the criticizing up to the coach.

The easiest way for someone to bring out the best in you is for you to bring out the best in them. Of course, there will always be that undesirable teammate. If his/her attitude or actions are detrimental to the team, try pulling that person aside and explaining what he/she may be doing wrong. Also suggest that he/she try making a change, because it will benefit the team as well as him/her. If that doesn't work, just keep communication to a minimum by just saying "hi" and "bye," this will prevent that individual from bringing your spirits down. Maintain a positive relationship with your teammates, if possible. Sometimes ask about their schoolwork and family. Most importantly, keep the team as a whole in prayer. If you conduct yourself with high standards and respect for everyone around you, it should not go unnoticed or unappreciated. Remember that:

Together
Everyone
Achieves
More

Opponents

Your true test of character and sportsmanship comes into play when you face your opposition. It is true that you train to compete and win, but while doing so you want to respect the opposing team and individual competitors. Greeting your opponents at the beginning of the game, playing by the rules and shaking hands at the end of the game will add flavor to any performance, regardless of the final score.

Do all you can to avoid any verbal and physical confrontations because a loud mouth and dirty play may lead to penalties and ejections. Furthermore, it may disrupt your team's overall performance. One problem with professional sports today is that the media and fans accept and sometimes encourage negative interactions between athletes. This hurts the integrity and enjoyment of sports. We should treat our opponents like we would want to be treated – with class and respect. Do all you can to leave that positive and competitive impression, because the opponent that you face today could very well be your teammate in the future.

On November 29, 1992 the New York Jets professional football team was playing the Kansas City Chiefs. Jets defensive end Dennis Byrd collided with one of his teammates, who was trying to make a tackle, and suffered a broken vertebra in his neck. As he laid on the field motionless while paramedics were attending to him, both teams immediately gathered at the middle of the field, took off their helmets, knelt down, held hands and prayed together. At that moment the score and everything else in that stadium was unimportant. When Dennis got to the hospital it was soon discovered that he was paralyzed from the waist down. Doctors had little hope for his recovery.

With heart and determination he pursued his rehabilitation with a vengeance. Three weeks after the injury he was able to walk with two canes. On opening day of the next season he walked out on the field, unassisted, to accept the Jets Most Inspirational player award, which was later renamed after him. Even though his playing career was over, he was so thankful that he was able to go on with his life. Despite all the medical personnel and treatment that was involved, he credits his teammates and *opponents*, who sent prayers up that day, for making the difference in his recovery.

Officials

Referees and umpires are essential and required for any approved athletic contest. Their job is to enforce the rules and safety of the respective game, match or meet. They are human and sometimes make mistakes. You could never pay me to be an official, because just about every close call involves scrutiny and criticism from athletes, coaches and fans alike.

Unfortunately, from Little League games in America to professional soccer matches in Europe, there have been officials seriously injured by unruly fans due to a judgment call. The sad thing is that games, no matter how emotionally charged at the time, do not have any bearing on anything in life. Regardless of the outcome, the sun will still rise the next day and life will still go on. No one's freedoms or life is at stake because an official makes a bad call. When an official makes an error he or she usually will have to answer to a higher authority eventually. If you are an athlete, accept whatever calls are made and live with it. If something is in question, it's the coach's responsibility to question it. In the end it may be changed or not repeated in the future.

You can easily win favor with officials by playing hard, playing fair and respecting their decisions. In most cases, if you consistently display these actions officials will usually give you a close call. If you feel the officials did call a good game or match, after the game let them know. Whether you win or lose, its says a lot about you as an athlete. It also makes them feel appreciated. However, if you weren't in agreement with their performance, the best thing to do is not to say anything to them. If you can't talk positive don't say anything, because it won't change anything. And, it could come back to haunt you if you meet again in the future.

During my junior year in high school, our junior varsity football team traveled to another school for a game. After both teams anxiously warmed up and got ready to play, it was soon discovered that there were *no* referees present. Unfortunately, the referees never did show up for that scheduled game so both teams had to pack it up and go home. Looking back on that day, there were about 80 disgruntled guys from both teams who worked hard all summer and wanted to play football but couldn't. I am convinced that if both teams had a choice that day, they both would have much rather played with mediocre or questionable officiating than not to have played at all.

Be A Class Act Off The Field

Chapter 7

Be a Class Act Off the Field

Let no man despise thy youth; but be thou an example of the believers, in word, in conversation, in charity, in spirit, in purity.
1 Timothy 4:12

Since school sports are extra-curricular activities you will obviously spend much more time off the playing field than on it. Your role in the community begins and never ends. It is the civic duty of every man, woman, boy, and girl to be a productive member of society. It is much more important to be a leader in your community, than being a superstar athlete. Leadership in the community will bring you greater rewards and will last longer.

Regardless of your age, everyone is in a position to serve and give back. If you are not old enough to be a registered voter, start by getting involved in student council or student government at your school. Be concerned with the concerns and opinions of your peers. Obey the law and encourage others to do the same. Never try to beat the system, but try to make the system work for you.

Volunteers are needed everywhere and will always be in demand. Participate in youth groups at your church, or, if there aren't any, talk to your pastor about starting one. Consider getting involved with the Fellowship of Christian Athletes, if there is a local chapter in your area (www.fca.org). Take opportunities to be a big brother or big sister to a lonely youth. Help out at Little League games by working concessions or keeping score. There may be students younger than you who need to be tutored in their schoolwork.

Years ago I had mentored a young boy at my church, who was in elementary school. We did lots of things together, such as bowling, going to football games and hanging out talking about any and everything. The years went by fast and we made a positive influence in each other's life. Today he is currently playing football on scholarship at a local college. He constantly thanks me for helping him get to where he is today.

Despite the negative images professional sports frequently portray, there are some Christian athletes who are still willing to take a stand for righteous living. A few for example are: football players, Shaun Alexander and Trent Dilfer; basketball players, David Robinson and Avery Johnson; baseball players, Mike Sweeney and Albert Pujols; Tennis player Michael Chang; soccer player Michele Akers; WNBA player Adrienne Johnson and NASCAR driver Jeff Gordon. These individuals are in a class by themselves, because they refuse to compromise morals and values for fame and fortune. If you sit down and talk with any of them, they would all agree that it is much better to live a testimony than to speak one.

American athletes seem to be in the media for more negative events than positive. From high school up to the professional ranks, its common to pick up the newspaper and read about athletes cheating on exams or committing violent crimes. One or two senseless athletes can give a whole group of athletes a bad name. It doesn't do a professional athlete any good to give a few thousand dollars to a charity, if they use drugs or have run-ins with the law. Professional basketball great Charles Barkley once did a commercial for Nike shoe company, stressing that he was not a role model because he was not paid to be a role model. He added, he was paid to play basketball and that children should look to their parents for role models.

What he is trying to explain, is that children need to look up to those who will feed and clothe them, be at their games and support all that they do. Professional athletes and celebrities will not be around to do these things for you, but parents will.

There are no perfect parents, but if you are blessed to have loving parents you should do all you can to honor them. Making your parents and family proud of you is the best gift you can possibly give to them. Being a positive person in all you do will help win the hearts of young and old. I constantly hear people say "everyone makes mistakes" and "what happens in the past stays in the past." These sayings are true, but they should not be an excuse to disobey the law or hurt those that mean the most to you.

If you're looking for an athletic role model, I have one for you. But, it's not Tiger Woods, Marion Jones or Cael Sanderson. A victim and a victor, Darryl Williams sets the example for all student-athletes. Although his playing days are long since over, few have given back or paid a higher price, than Darryl Williams.

His athletic experiences had to be applied to the game of life at a young age. Having survived a life-threatening situation, he has since become a voice for the human rights of all people. Darryl was a tenth grader from Roxbury, Massachusetts making his first varsity football start. He caught a pass that gave his Jamaica Plain High School, a 6-0 halftime lead over Charlestown High. September, 1979 seemed like a good time for Darryl. He hoped to someday go to the NFL. As the Jamaica Plain football team gathered in a huddle before the second half, a sniper's bullet finished his dreams. Darryl's career was over, but at least his life was spared. His fate that day was attributed to a hate crime resulting from court ordered busing in Boston, Massachusetts.

After the attack, which left him without the use of his arms and legs, and after all the broken promises of medical and financial support, Darryl looks at life in a way that surprises most people. Despite being the victim of a hate crime, he harbors no bitterness toward any other race. He feels there are good and bad people in every race. Having paid a heavy price for his status, Darryl brings his inspiring message to thousands of Americans. Many are student-athletes, who come to realize how quickly the sports dream can end. But that is not what Darryl communicates to them. His very existence symbolizes hope for meaningful life after sports.

Darryl later received a scholarship to Northeastern University and is now employed by the Massachusetts State Lottery. Despite all the adversity that took place, he still feels blessed and refuses to let a day go by without reaching out and inspiring others. Darryl Williams, because of all you suffered and overcame, you're my hero!

A lapse of judgment can destroy a good name and years of hard work. I know of individuals who made one mistake and ended up losing scholarships, careers and even their freedom. I once heard a minister say, "an idle mind is the devil's workshop," so it's best to keep your life occupied with positive things and positive people. Positive people can help get you where you want to go and bring out the best in you. Don't be a victim of peer pressure. Make it a priority to associate with peers who have high moral standards. Choose to be with peers who honor parents, respect authority and value education.

In 1999 I took a youth group from my church to an inspirational fellowship. The keynote speaker was Dave Meyer, who was a quarterback at Virginia Tech University. He was also involved in various on campus ministries and was the backup for All-Pro Michael Vick of the Atlanta Falcons. He consistently stressed to the group how important it was to pick and choose friends wisely, because it will drastically affect your future. He concluded by saying. "If you choose to hang around garbage, you're eventually going to smell like it."

The recent sexual assault allegations of professional basketball player Kobe Bryant should send out a message to all student-athletes on the importance of high morals and good conduct. Despite his claims of having consensual sex with his accuser, his bad decision making will cost him his public respect, bring shame to his family and the loss of millions of dollars in earnings. Be smart, do the right thing in all situations. If a situation doesn't look right or feel right, chances are it isn't. Walk away. Your future depends on it.

In recent years I have served as a volunteer at the Salvation Army and a church soup kitchen. These experiences opened my eyes to a lot and I feel that every warm blooded American should have these experiences. I was surprised how many people in this country are living in poverty. There are many people who are thankful just to get a hot meal everyday, no matter where it comes from. There are some that go to bed every night without electricity or running water. Even though it hurts to see these types of circumstances, we all should appreciate all that we do have. You can't save the world. But, if you try to make a difference in one person's life, it will eventually spread.

It is a fact that many less fortunate people were well-to-do at one time, so it can happen to anyone at any time. There are many Americans, who are one or two paychecks away from being homeless. If you choose to serve in any volunteer capacity, you will soon discover that it will bring more joy than any goal scored or homerun hit.

Outstanding opportunities to help others seldom come: Small ones come every day.

Make etiquette a part of your everyday lifestyle. Etiquette is defined in Webster's dictionary as common, everyday courtesy. Society as a whole functions more smoothly and pleasantly when people practice good manners. Respect all those that you come in contact with, such as those less fortunate, the handicap and especially the elderly. Saying "yes Sir and no Ma'am" will make your elders appreciate you and bring back the respectability that today's youth have lost over the years. Simple things like saying "please" and "thank you" will help any organization run smoother, because people respond more enthusiastically when asked in a courteous manner to do something. They will also appreciate knowing their efforts are recognized when told "thank you."

One of the most valuable habits anyone can develop is to be on time. Whether it is getting to school, church or appointments being on time says a lot about your commitment and responsibility. Obviously, there are times when a person cannot avoid being late. When practical, it is best to call ahead to let people know you'll be late or reschedule the appointment. Do not keep people waiting on the phone. If you can't help them right away, offer to return the call later or write down a message and pass it along to those who can.

You should never feel people have to speak to you first before you to speak to them. Being the first to greet someone you know, or even a stranger, offers a positive impression of you. Taking time out each day to greet or speak to someone could be what that person needs, especially if they are not having the best day. Remember, it doesn't cost you anything. As the Bible states, "Don't forget to entertain strangers, for by doing some people have entertained angels without knowing it" (Hebrews 13:2). What this scripture means is that people you don't know can be sent into our lives at any time to be blessed by you.

Don't gossip. A discussion of others' personal habits, problems, and activities, true or untrue, often results in quarrels and disputes. The morale of any organization may suffer because of feuds that arise from gossip. The best policy is not to gossip and to discourage others from gossiping.

Strive to be a person of integrity. Integrity simply means doing the right thing when no one is looking. Integrity is not cheating on exams. Integrity is driving the speed limit. Integrity is returning extra money to a cashier who gave you too much change. By doing so you may save that person's job, because someone has to answer for the loss.

I once went to a gym with a coworker who found a wallet as we were leaving. He didn't check the contents and immediately turned it in at the front desk without leaving any information about himself. When I asked him what inspired his honesty, he said that the money in the wallet could have been needed to buy groceries for someone's children or gas for someone to get back and forth to work. He chose to do the right thing, because he didn't want to live with the wrong decision on his conscience.

As a teenager and adult, there will be times when employment is required to provide for your needs and wants. When you are working a part-time or summer job, try to be the best employee possible. Whether you are mowing lawns, bagging groceries or serving fast foods, it is your moral obligation to give your employer at least 100% every time you show up for work. Every employer thrives off of having a model employee. Model employees finish what they have to do, than go help someone else. Model employees try to keep peace and harmony during hectic situations. Model employees will honor an employer's rules and policies by not lying, cheating or stealing.

My pastor, Rev. E.D. Richardson, consistently stresses that Christian employees must set the standard by giving total dedication and commitment. Prior to his calling to the full-time ministry, he spent 22 years building ships for the U.S. Navy. During his tenure he said he saw employees spending more time and energy avoiding and dodging work, and disrupting others, when they could have used less energy getting the job done. Staying busy on the job makes the day go by faster and the job go smoother.

If you are an employee who chooses to go above and beyond, you may be able to get a job anywhere in this country. The rewards of being a model employee are numerous, such as being promoted to better positions in the present and future. If you are a summer hire, being a model employee could motivate an employer to rehire you for the next summer. Finally, it leaves a positive impression for those, who come along after you, as well as gives you the confidence and desire to pursue bigger challenges in the future.

"The time is always right to do the right thing".
-Martin Luther King, Jr-

When The Game Is Over Move On

Chapter 8

When the Game is Over Move On

Trust in the Lord with all your heart and lean not on your own understanding; in all your ways acknowledge him, and he will direct your paths.

Proverbs 3:5-6

You know by now preparation is essential for any type of success. Preparation for life after sports is of the utmost importance, but occasionally can be overlooked. The previous chapter went into brief detail about a student-athlete's role off the field. Finally, there will be a time when your athletic career will come to a complete end. This is sad, but a reality.

Since the odds of making it to the professional ranks are so high, most student-athlete must make plans for life well before the balls stop bouncing and the bats stop swinging. Some high school athletes will be fortunate to go to college, while others will not. Some athletes will make it to college, but will choose not to play sports due to the academic challenges that they will face. Regardless of the course in life you choose to follow as a student-athlete, you must accept the fact that the more important things in life will be there when sports are over and gone.

Today there are many professional sports franchises that offer mentoring and transitional education programs for athletes who are facing retirement. These programs were established because many former professional athletes have fallen on hard times after leaving their respective sports. In the past some former professional athletes had to resort to minimum wage jobs or fell victim to drugs and alcohol simply because they did not adequately prepare for life after their playing days were over.

Transitional education programs have been recently adopted by some major Division I colleges due to low student-athlete graduation rates. Student-athletes are leaving colleges in droves without being able to do anything but play sports. Since college athletics are now multi-million dollar enterprises, athletes are being showered with temporary fame and attention, which they can't do anything with when it's time to move on.

Your career and life long ambitions should begin to take shape in high school and continue the rest of your life.
He who fails to plan – plans to fail is an old proverb that is still true today.

To make good career decisions and plans, you need as much information as possible. Strive at every moment to learn more about yourself and career opportunities. This will prepare you to choose the career that is right for you. Don't pursue something because of the money or because it's what family and friends think you should do. If you are digging ditches because it pays $20 a hour and it's not want you want, than you are going to be miserable every day you go to work. If mom and dad want you to become an accountant and you know that you don't like sitting in an office playing with numbers all day, than you will not last long in that profession.

You should begin to explore career fields when you are in middle school and high school. If opportunities present themselves, you can become involved in activities related to your career interests. Additionally, read about your career interest and talk with those already working in that field. At the high school level, continue to think about your life and career goals. To do this you should determine your aptitudes, interests, personal characteristics and values by consulting teachers and guidance counselors. Most workers are happiest and most successful when their jobs match their strengths, personality and beliefs.

The kind of career you have can affect your life in many ways. For example, it can determine where you live, the friends you make, and the amount of money you earn. Your career can determine how well you feel about yourself and the way other people act towards you. By making wise decisions concerning your career, you can help yourself enjoy the life you want.

"If all athletes were to give school as much of their concentration as do potential doctors, lawyers or businessmen, there wouldn't be any problems for ex-stars, who were careless with their studies and, as a consequence, unsuccessful in life at the conclusion of their careers."

-Michael Johnson-
Three-time Olympic Gold Medalist
Nine-time World Track and Field Champion

Sometimes you may change careers, at least a couple times, before finally finding your niche. For example, after a very successful college basketball career at Providence College, Billy Donovan lasted a year in the NBA before moving on to Wall Street with his marketing degree in hand. After a year on Wall Street he soon realized that trying to sell investments to people wasn't for him. He kept in contact with his college coach and mentor Rick Pitino, who had later moved on to the University of Kentucky. He explained to Coach Pitino how unhappy he was and how much he had missed being around the game. Coach Pitino soon offered him a graduate assistant coach position, which paid very little, but it would eventually lead to higher positions.

Billy immediately took advantage of the opportunity, studied the game and learned what it took to coach a nationally ranked program. His persistence and patience paid off. Five years later he was offered the head coaching job at Marshall University. While at Marshall he resurrected a losing program, while compiling winning records each of the two seasons he was there. Since taking over the program at University of Florida in 1996, his teams have been to the post season every year and he is currently one of the winningest active college coaches. Not to mention that he currently has a 90% graduation rate and has placed 26 players on the Southeast Conference Honor Roll, including a league record six in 1997 and 1998. He is changing young men's lives for the better, doing what he loves and was recently rewarded with a lucrative contract extension.

During an interview for *Sharing the Victory* magazine, he stated "When I got cut from the Knicks, it was devastating. But God opened up another door for me to go into coaching. I look back on it now and realize, 'Maybe that pain I went through was because God had a different plan for me.' If you try to put your trust in Him in the way you're going, you try to lead your life each and every day in the right manner. You may get more pleasure out of that than at the previous place you were."

There is so much more to life than grueling practices and nagging injuries. You may know people who were excellent high school or college athletes that like to consistently talk about their glory days in the past. It might sound interesting at first, but eventually it gets old. In my home office I have a shelf with trophies and plaques I have accumulated over the years. As exciting as it once was winning them, I can't do anything with them now but watch them collect dust. A few years ago I had a conversation with a friend, who was a former college athlete. He said it would be nice if he could take one of his trophies to the store and exchange it for a loaf of bread, then it would have been worth all the effort of winning it.

Toward the end of my military career I was playing in a basketball league for men over 30 years old. It came down to the last game of the season, which my team needed to win in order to advance to the playoffs. My team played a hard fought game, but unfortunately lost in the end. For me the feeling was bittersweet because even though we didn't make the playoffs, my body was wracked with pain from head to toe. I was definitely looking forward to the rest and recuperation, which I desperately needed.

After shaking hands and wishing the other team good luck in the playoffs, I noticed a gentleman on the floor shooting and making baskets—*from a wheelchair!* From talking to a couple of people I learned that the person had become a paraplegic as the result of being in a plane crash. I also learned that he was the leading scorer for his traveling wheelchair basketball team, as well as a local advocate for the physically disabled. Just seeing him enjoying making shot after shot unassisted, brought tears to my eyes. He very easily could have taken the easy way out by feeling sorry for himself and being a burden on society, but instead he chose to move on and enjoy life.

On my way to the locker room, I stopped to tell him that my team sure could have used him during the game we had just lost. He said 'thanks' as he continued sinking shots. Sometimes we just don't know how blessed we really are.

Before his untimely death at age 50, Reginald Lewis would make his mark as one of the most savvy and dynamic businessmen of his generation. After a stellar high school career, Lewis earned a football scholarship to Virginia State University, unfortunately a shoulder injury shelved his career as a quarterback. Lewis had struggled in the classroom early on. But with football pushed aside, he began applying commitment and sacrifice toward his books and earned a degree in economics. During a summer orientation at Harvard Law School, he so impressed professors there that he was granted admission without taking the entrance exam.

He finished Harvard in 1968 and began practicing law in Manhattan. By 1983 he had set up the TLC Group so he could buy and sell companies. In his first major deal he bought a struggling company for $22.5 million, restored it to financial health and sold it four years later for $90 million. Lewis had used an unexpected setback in his athletic career as a foundation for building one of the nation's largest business empires, with revenues of more than $1 billion.

"Three grand essentials for happiness in this life are something to do, someone to love, and something to hope for."
-Addison-

Regardless of how good or bad your athletic career turned out, you have to let it go and move on. Whether you were an All-American or a reserve you must move on. Be thankful for the ability, if not the opportunity. When I played football and basketball in high school the teams would recite the Lord's Prayer after every practice and game. The purpose of this was to give thanks to the Lord for the ability to play and compete. There are thousands of children in countries around the world who cannot participate in sports because of civil wars and social unrest. There are thousands of children in the United States who desire to participate in sports, but cannot because they are blind or handicapped. Just weighing those reasons alone is more than enough to give thanks.

I once heard Pastor John Hagee of Cornerstone Christian Center in San Antonio, Texas preach a sermon on gratitude. He said, "no matter who you are or where you are there is always going to be someone better. There will always be someone who will look better. There will always be someone who can do something better than others. There is always someone who is a better doctor, lawyer or mechanic. If you want to be happy just be the best you can possibly be and forget about the rest."

Always strive to avoid monotony and stagnation in your life. Be open and be willing to try new ideas and interests, such as woodworking, writing short stories or learning how to play a musical instrument. Don't rule out anything until you try it at least once or twice. I tried fishing for the first time twelve years ago and fell in love with it. It's a good way to relax and enjoy the outdoors God created. Nothing ventured is nothing gained. Remember this – the Ark was built by amateurs, the Titanic was built by professionals.

-Variety is the spice of life-

Throughout my life I have attended many funerals of family and friends. Some of the deceased were good athletes at one time in their lives and were cited for such notable things while they were living. But I have never read an obituary or heard a eulogy that mentioned how many homeruns a person hit, how many touchdowns a person scored or how many races a person won. How you live your life and what you do for others determines what will be said about you after you have passed. It is everyone's duty to live a life of honor and praise.

In conclusion, use that same desire and effort that you display running races, shooting baskets and hitting homeruns to enhance your career and relationships, because these are the things which make this country great and life worth living. With the Lord's blessing and the combined efforts of everyone, you can help to put an end to the "dumb jock troublemaker" image. Student-athletes can be faithful servants of honor and respect.

"We make a living by what we get, we make a life by what we give."

-Sir Winston Churchill-

Athlete's Prayer

Help me to play the game, dear Lord, with all my might and main;
Grant me the courage born of right, a heart to stand the strain…

Send me a sense of humor, Lord, to laugh when victory's mine;
To laugh, if I should meet, without a fret or whine…

Give me the grace to follow rules, to 'fess up when I'm wrong',
When silence or some other thing wins plaudits from the throng…

When foes are tough and fighting fierce and I am getting weak,
Dear God, don't ever let me show a broad, bright, yellow streak.

And teach me, Lord, life's game to play just one day at a time.
With Thee as coach and trainer, Lord, real victory must be mine.

Selected References

Chapter 1

1. Sports Illustrated, March 9, 1992, v 76 n 9
2. Title IX: 25 Years of Progress, U. S. Department of Education, June 1997

Chapter 2

1. Indianapolis Star, April 12, 2001

Chapter 3

1. Homework Success, Oregon Department of Education, 1999
2. There's More to Life, Danny Wuerffel, October 2000

Chapter 4

1. The Sports Success Book, Karl Marrow Woods, 1985

Chapter 5

1. Think and Grow Rich: A Black Choice, Dennis Kimbro, 1991
2. Coaching Wrestling Successfully, Dan Gable, 1998
3. All Things Possible, Kurt Warner, 2001

Chapter 6

1. Reach for the Summit, Pat Summitt, 1999
2. Rise and Walk, Dennis Byrd, 1993

Chapter 7

1. The Boston Globe, February 6, 2001

Chapter 8

1. Sharing the Victory, December 30, 2002
2. Richmond Times–Dispatch, February 1, 2002
3. Michael Johnson: sprinter deluxe, Bert Rosenthal, 2000

Dual Role Order Form

Use this convenient order form to order additional copies of
Dual Role

Please Print:

Name____

Address______________________________________

City______________________ **State**______________

Zip________________

Phone(   )_______________________

_____ copies of book @ $6.99 each $ ________

Postage and handling @ $2.00 per book $ ________

Total amount enclosed $ ________

Make checks payable to Elwood Scales III

Send to Elwood Scales III
P. O. Box 64 • Hampton, VA 23669